Money Conscious Cookbook: Easy and Delicious Recipes for Your Taste Buds and Your Wallet to Enjoy

Table of Contents

Laundry Detergent (Total Cost $3 vs. $12)

Ingredients:
- 1 C borax
- 1 C Washing Soda
- 1 bar of soap

Directions:

I.   Grate the soap over a mixing bowl
II.   Add in your borax, stirring
III.   Slowly stir in your washing soda
IV.   Store in air tight container
   ** Use 1 T per washing load

Ingredients:

- 1-2 lbs. apples

Directions:

I. Add apple cores and peels to pie pans with ¼ C sugar to each pie pan

II. Cover the pans with a towel or loose over for about 1-2 weeks

III. Scoop away any mold that may have developed and pour vinegar into mason jars and tighten lids

Ingredients:
- ½ Corn starch
- ½ C green clay
- ½ C cocoa

Directions:

I.   Mix everything together and store in air tight container like a mason jar or baby food jar

All Natural Bug spray

Ingredients:
- 40 drops essential oil of your choice
- 50 drops coconut oil

Directions:

I.   Blend the two oils and store in small container

Cough Syrup

Ingredients:
- 4 C water
- ¼ C dried elderberries
- 2 T dried elder flowers
- 2 T dried plantain leaf
- ½ C honey

Directions:

I.   Add water, flowers, berries and plantain to pan and bring to a boil

II.   Let simmer for around 12-15 minutes after short rolling boil.

III.   Add saucepan to oven to let steep for around 2 hours or so, then strain

IV.   Add infusion back in pan after straining water, throwing away the herbs (or composting)

V.   Lower heat on stove to low or preheat (I do this when I don't want it to cook really hot)

VI.   Remove pan, and add honey while still warm

VII.   Store in air tight container and this is good for about 1-3 months

Chest Vapor Rub

Ingredients:
- ½ C olive oil
- 1 C coconut oil
- ¾ C grated beeswax
- 35 eucalyptus drops
- 35 drops mint oil
- 12 drops lavender drops
- 10 drops rosemary drops
- 10 drops camphor oil

Directions:

I. Melt the wax over a double broiler with the oils and stir well, stir in the essential oils and pour into small molds

Vacuum Carpet powder

Ingredients:
- 1 ½ C baking soda
- Cinnamon essential oils

Directions:

I.   Mix the two ingredients together and store in a mason jar or like container

Personal Lip Balm (cost $2)

Ingredients:
- 2 T Beeswax
- 2 T shea butter
- 2 T coconut oil

Directions:

I. Melt the three ingredients together and add drops of desired essential oils,
II. Let set until hardens

Homemade Dry shampoo (cost $3)

Ingredients:

- 1 C warm water
- ¼ C arrowroot
- ¼ C witch hazel, or alcohol

Directions:

I.   Add the ingredients together and store in air tight container and apply with blush brush or large tooth comb

Coconut Toothpaste (cost $1 vs. $4)

Ingredients:
- 1 T coconut oil
- 2 T xylitol
- 1 T baking soda
- 16-33 drops peppermint oil

Directions:

I.   Mix everything together and add to a container with a lid.

Jewelry Cleaner ($4 vs. $10)

Ingredients:
- 1 T salt
- 1 T baking soda
- 1 T dish detergent
- 1 C water
- Aluminum foil

Directions:

I.   Heat the water in your microwave and add press foil down into bottom o bowl (AFTER HEATING DO NOT ADD FOIL TO MICROWAVE-Obviously)

II. Add hot water to bowl, and add remaining ingredients

III. Place jewelry to bottom on bowl and let sit for a few minutes, around 10 minutes

IV. Rinse jewelry and throw away cleaner

V.   You will need to mix this together for each time you need to clean your jewelry

Ingredients:

- 1 roll paper towels
- 4 C water
- 1 T coconut oil
- 1 tsp all natural cleaning wash

Directions:

I. Cut down the paper towel roll to half, and add our other ingredients to a mixing bowl or measuring cup. * Make these when ready to use.
II. Heat liquids in bowl
III. When ready to use, soak your paper towel roll into the bowl with cleanser

True All Natural Body Wash ($2 vs $6)

Ingredients:

- Castile soap, grated
- 12 C water
- 2 T glycerin

Directions:

I. Simmer the water and add soap, making sure it is completely melted
II. Remove from heat and add glycerin
III. Cover and let set for 24 hours before using

Ingredients:

- 3 T powdered ginger
- 1 coffee mug full of boiling water
- 3 C Epsom salts

Directions:

I.   Run tub of water, and salts and
II.   stir ginger in (do not get IN the tub yet) the Drinkable (BUT boiling hot water) let ginger dissolve,
III.   Drink the water quickly
IV.   Get in the tub to your neck and set.

Liver Detox Smoothie

Ingredients:

- 3-4 beets, sliced
- 3 sliced carrots
- 2 C Kale
- 1 C dandelion greens
- 1 lemon, wedged
- 1 apple, cored and sliced
- 1 C purple cabbage, chopped
- Water
- 2 T MCT oil

Directions:

I. Add everything into your blender and blend, if needed do this in smaller portions, them blend everything together
II. When liquid, drink and enjoy

Peppermint Tea

Ingredients:
- 1 bag herbal peppermint tea
- 1 C boiled water

Directions:

I. Steep your tea
II. Drink tea hot, after dinner

Tummy Tamer

Ingredients:
I.   1 fresh gingerroot
II.   Grater
III.   1 C boiling water
IV.   Honey and lemon to garnish

Directions:

I.   Wash and grate your ginger and add boiling water over grated ginger
II.   Add boiling water over ginger

Ingredients:
- ¼ tsp cayenne powder
- 4 oz. water

Directions:

I. Mix the two ingredients and soak a cotton ball or similar object and swab the inside of your nose, you want to FEEL the heat from the cayenne pepper. This is a great headache killer.

Flowers For Migraines

Ingredients:
- 1 Oz. dried flowers
- 1 pint boiling water

Directions:

I.   Blend 1 oz. of flowers per 1 pint boiling water, and steep. Drink ½ a C twice a day for migraines

Ingredients:
- ¼ C ACV
- 3-4 C boiling water
- 1 C cool water

Directions:

I. ¼ C apple cider vinegar with ½ of the boiling water, add a towel over your head and lean over the bowl of boiling water

Ingredients:

- 1 T fish oil
- 8 oz. orange juice

Directions:

I.   Just add the T of fish oil to the orange juice and stir well.
II. Enjoy and drink your orange juice

Sneak Peak to Kids treats in Book II.

Ingredients:

- 2 C coconut milk
- 2 frozen bananas
- ½ tsp salt
- 1 C frozen liver, chopped
- 1 C frozen berries
- 1 C Kale
- 1 ½ C ice
- 1 T chia seeds

Directions:

I.   Add everything to your blender or food processor and blend until smooth

Ingredients:
- 1 ¼ C tart cherry juice
- 4 T gelatin
- ¼ C elderberry Syrup
- 2 T raw honey

Directions:

I.   Bring Juice to a boil and pour into a glass mixing bowl with the gelatin, stirring or whisking
II.   Stir in the rest of the ingredients, and whisk until well combined
III. Pour mixture into small bite size molds and let set in fridge for 2-4 hours
IV.   Serve and enjoy

Chocolate minty popsicles

Ingredients:
- 1 C coconut milk
- 2 bananas
- 4 T cocoa powder
- 1 T coconut sugar
- 1 tsp vanilla
- Salt
- 3 drops peppermint oil (essential oil)

Directions:

I. Add everything in to your blender but the peppermint oil and blend well

II. Add in the peppermint drop and blend for another 8-10 seconds

III. Pour mixture into the molds and freeze until completely frozen

Sunburn Spray

Ingredients:

- ½ C water
- 2 T pure aloe Vera gel
- 10-12 drops lavender essential oils
- 10 drops peppermint essential oils
- Small spray bottle

Directions:

I. Blend all of your ingredients in a small spray bottle and apply as needed

www.ingramcontent.com/pod-product-compliance
Lightning Source LLC
Chambersburg PA
CBHW070756180526
45168CB00004B/1643